On the Job

Contractors

Perimeter and Area

Rane Anderson

Consultants

Michele Ogden, Ed.D
Principal, Irvine Unified School District

Jennifer Robertson, M.A.Ed.
Teacher, Huntington Beach City School District

Publishing Credits

Rachelle Cracchiolo, M.S.Ed., *Publisher*
Conni Medina, M.A.Ed., *Managing Editor*
Dona Herweck Rice, *Series Developer*
Emily R. Smith, M.A.Ed., *Series Developer*
Diana Kenney, M.A.Ed., NBCT, *Content Director*
Stacy Monsman, M.A., *Editor*
Kevin Panter, *Graphic Designer*

Image Credits: All images from iStock and/or
Shutterstock.

Teacher Created Materials

5301 Oceanus Drive
Huntington Beach, CA 92649-1030
http://www.tcmpub.com

ISBN 978-1-4807-5811-7
© 2018 Teacher Created Materials, Inc.
Made in China
Nordica.022017.CA21700227

Table of Contents

Build It, Fix It

Contractors are go-to people for anyone who wants to **renovate** an indoor or outdoor space. You can find them on any construction project, big or small. It is the contractor's job to bring ideas to life.

Some **clients** have unique requests. They want houses made from glass bottles and walls made from tires. They want houses built in trees and rooms hidden behind bookcases. Regardless of the request, contractors find ways to get the work done.

Most of the time, clients have much simpler requests. They might ask for a new kitchen countertop. They might need a new backyard fence. In either case, contractors are there to help. They measure spaces, buy supplies, use tools to fix problems. They might even hire other skilled workers to help. Contractors work hard to make dreams come true.

plans for a kitchen remodel

The David Wenzel Treehouse at Nay Aug Park in Pennsylvania, overlooks a gorge from 150 feet (46 meters) above.

Prepping for the Job

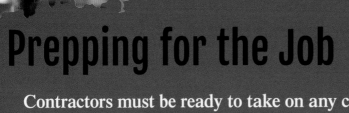

Contractors must be ready to take on any challenge. One frequent request from clients is deck repair. First, contractors must gather information and plan what they want to do. That means they must inspect the space. By doing so, contractors can figure out the exact repairs that must be done.

Perhaps the wood is in good shape, but the paint is old. In that case, **refinishing** might be the answer. Or, a few boards might be damaged. Those can be replaced. If too many boards need to be replaced, a contractor might suggest building a new deck in its place. Perhaps the deck appears unstable. No one wants a deck to collapse while they are standing on it! In this instance, the deck's braces and posts must be checked. Contractors will then decide the best way to fix the problem.

unsafe deck

new safe deck

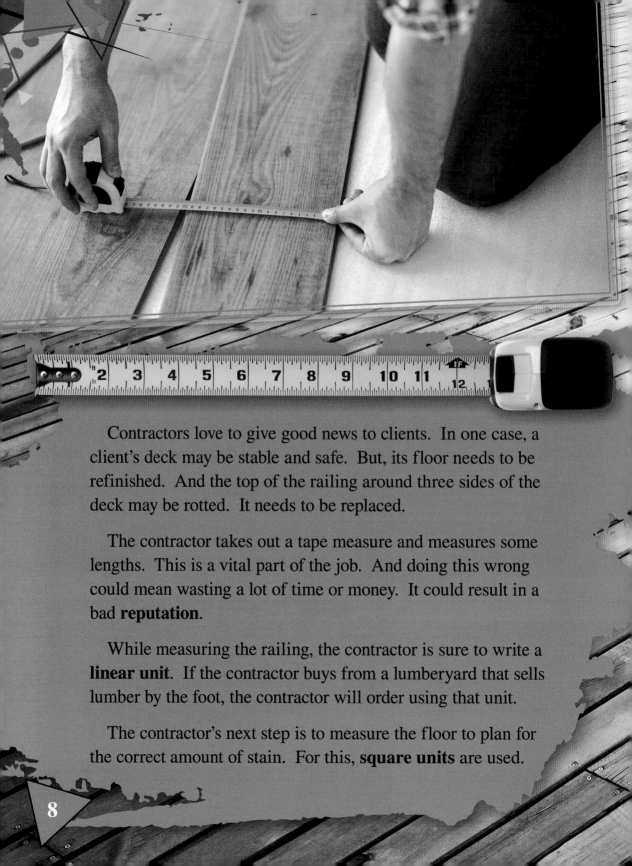

Contractors love to give good news to clients. In one case, a client's deck may be stable and safe. But, its floor needs to be refinished. And the top of the railing around three sides of the deck may be rotted. It needs to be replaced.

The contractor takes out a tape measure and measures some lengths. This is a vital part of the job. And doing this wrong could mean wasting a lot of time or money. It could result in a bad **reputation**.

While measuring the railing, the contractor is sure to write a **linear unit**. If the contractor buys from a lumberyard that sells lumber by the foot, the contractor will order using that unit.

The contractor's next step is to measure the floor to plan for the correct amount of stain. For this, **square units** are used.

While preparing an **estimate**, a contractor sketches a deck so that needed measurements can be recorded. One side of the deck does not need a railing because the house is there.

1. How many feet of lumber does the contractor need to buy for the railing?

2. How many square feet of the deck's floor will need to be covered by stain?

3. What is the difference between the linear units used to measure the railing and the square units used to measure the floor?

12 ft.

10 ft.

10 ft.

House

Contractors use math every day. They add, subtract, multiply, and divide. They also have to find the **perimeter** and **area** of spaces. *Perimeter* is a word with Greek roots. *Peri* means "around," and *metron* means "measure." So, it makes sense that the distance around the outside of a shape is called the perimeter.

When contractors need to find out how much railing a deck should have, they must measure the perimeter. They measure the distance around the deck. Once the lengths and widths are known, they are added together. This is the perimeter of the deck.

perimeter

area

But what if a contractor wants to refinish a deck's floor? Do they measure the perimeter? No, this is when finding area can help. Area is the amount of space on the surface of a shape or place. If a client's deck is a rectangle, the contractor must find the length and width first. Then, the length and width can be used to find the area of the deck.

Finding the perimeter and area of a space can help a contractor save time and money by doing the project right the first time.

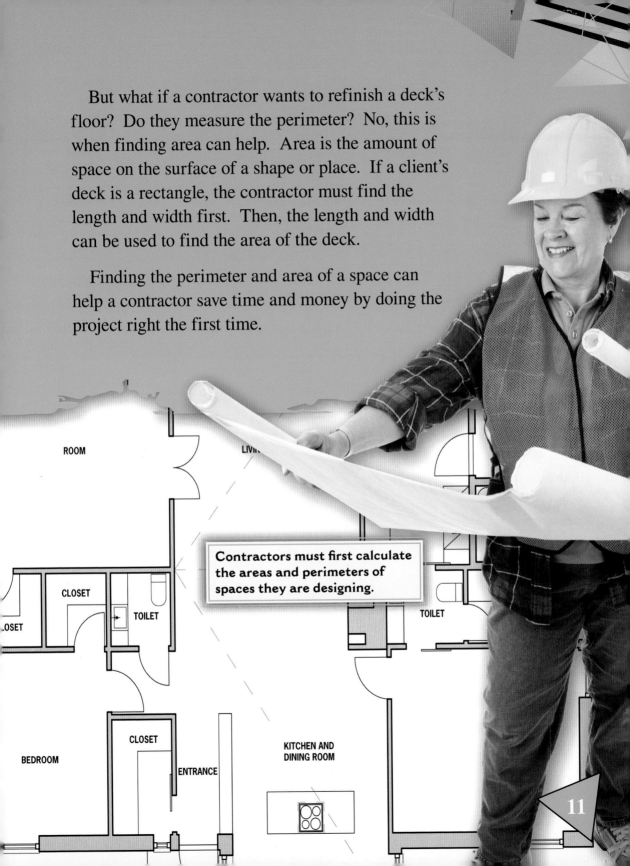

ROOM

LIVI...

CLOSET

TOILET

.OSET

TOILET

Contractors must first calculate the areas and perimeters of spaces they are designing.

CLOSET

BEDROOM

ENTRANCE

KITCHEN AND DINING ROOM

Estimate

Angel Silva
Silva Construction

SILVA CONSTRUCTION

Project

Banks Renovation

Customer

Doug Banks

Project scope: renovate kitchen, install new appliances, fix plumbing issues in master bathroom

Description	Qty	Units	Material	Labor	Subcontractor	Cost
						562.50
Phase 1: Demolition						562.50
Kitchen					562.50	562.50
Remove kitchen cabinets	1	Each	0.00	0.00		
Donate to charity						5,100.00
Phase 2: Construction						4,575.00
Kitchen						550.00
Appliances						550.00
Dishwasher	1	Each	400.00	150.00	0.00	
						3,437.50
Cabinetry					0.00	937.50
Granite countertop	25	SF	625.00	312.50		2,500.00
Kitchen cabinets	1	Each	0.00	0.00	2,500.00	587.50
Flooring						587.50
Refinish hardwood floor	200	SF	125.00	462.50	0.00	
						525.00
Master Bathroom						525.00
Plumbing						525.00
Replace bathtub	1	Each	375.00	150.00	0.00	
						375.00
Phase 3: Cleanup					375.00	375.00
General cleaning	1500	SF	0.00	0.00		
Project Total			1,525.00	1,075.00	3,437.50	6,037.50
					Tax	301.89
					Total with Tax	6,339.39

Accepted By: _____ Date:_____ Silva Construction: _____

12

Before clients will hire anyone to work on a deck, they will want to see a **bid**. A bid is a written estimate of all the costs for a project. Clients might ask for bids from a lot of contractors. They want to find the best price.

Placing bids can be tricky. If a bid is too low, the contractor will not make money from the job. But if a bid is too high, the clients might choose someone else to do the work. Being precise when adding **expenses** helps contractors write accurate bids.

Expenses are the costs of the job. Contractors must answer many questions to figure out costs. What materials are needed? Are permits required? How many workers are needed? All of these things have to be carefully considered before placing a bid.

Once contractors figure out the total cost, they can submit bids to clients. Then, they wait. If they got it right, they will be chosen for the project!

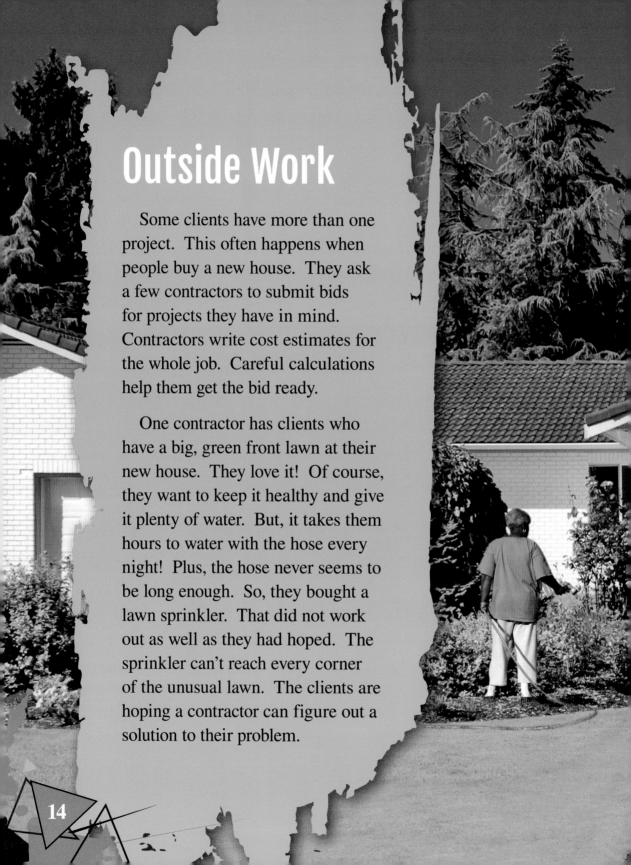

Outside Work

Some clients have more than one project. This often happens when people buy a new house. They ask a few contractors to submit bids for projects they have in mind. Contractors write cost estimates for the whole job. Careful calculations help them get the bid ready.

One contractor has clients who have a big, green front lawn at their new house. They love it! Of course, they want to keep it healthy and give it plenty of water. But, it takes them hours to water with the hose every night! Plus, the hose never seems to be long enough. So, they bought a lawn sprinkler. That did not work out as well as they had hoped. The sprinkler can't reach every corner of the unusual lawn. The clients are hoping a contractor can figure out a solution to their problem.

The contractor studies the lawn. It looks like the best option is to install a sprinkler system. The system will start on a timer. The sprinklers will turn on at a certain time each night.

The contractor tells the clients his plan. They are excited! Now, they won't have to fight the hose that is always too short. They won't have to move the sprinkler throughout the day. This sounds like the best option. With a sprinkler system, the yard will always look fresh and lush.

To make the system work, pipes will have to be placed underground and around the outside of the lawn. These pipes will take water to the sprinkler heads. The contractor needs to figure out how much pipe to buy.

Step 1: Lay underground pipes.

Step 2: Cut pipes to attach the sprinkler heads.

Step 3: Attach sprinkler heads to pipes.

1. What is the perimeter of the lawn?

2. How is finding the perimeter of this lawn different from finding the perimeter of a rectangle? How is it similar?

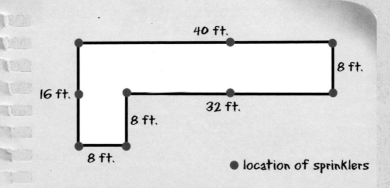

40 ft.

8 ft.

16 ft.

32 ft.

8 ft.

8 ft.

● location of sprinklers

Inside Work

The clients love the plan for their new sprinkler system. They are excited to see their lawn grow to a beautiful, crisp green color. But now, they have a second job for the bid. The color of their dining room is getting on their nerves. The color is too bright and distracting. The clients decide they want a totally new color on the wall. So, they ask a contractor for help.

The contractor wants to know what color the clients want for their dining room. The clients like the natural colors they now see in their front yard. They decide they want a more natural color.

Now that the contractor knows which color to buy, it is time to figure out how much of the wall will need paint. Then, the right amount of paint can be purchased. Finding the area of the wall will help.

paint sample swatches

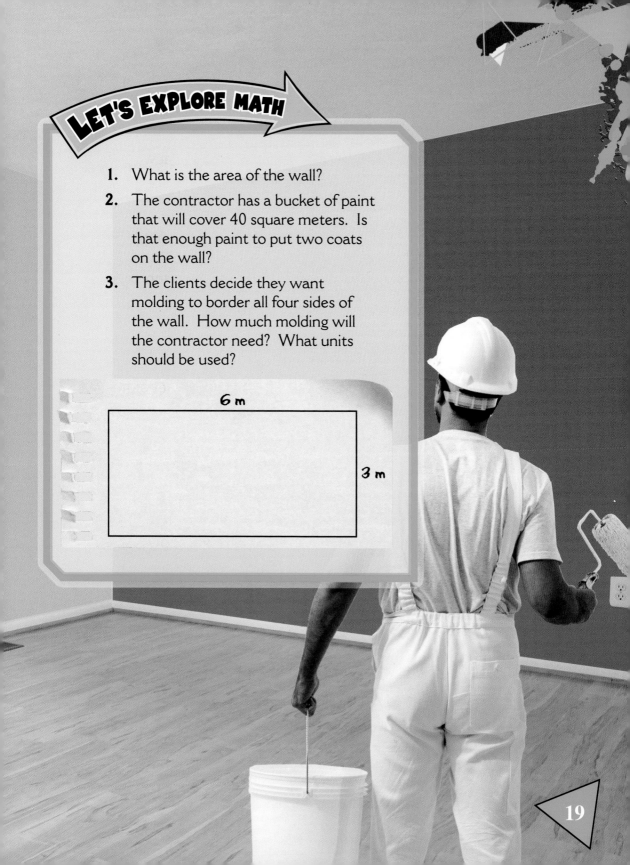

LET'S EXPLORE MATH

1. What is the area of the wall?

2. The contractor has a bucket of paint that will cover 40 square meters. Is that enough paint to put two coats on the wall?

3. The clients decide they want molding to border all four sides of the wall. How much molding will the contractor need? What units should be used?

6 m

3 m

The plan for the dining room is perfect! The natural walls will look beautiful as people eat their meals. But now, the carpet in the living room looks old and out of place! The contractor is happy to add a third job to the bid. The first step will be to measure the living room floor.

The living room floor is shaped like a rectangle. First, the contractor must find an accurate length and width. These measurements will help determine the amount of carpet and baseboard that is needed.

After finding the area and perimeter, the contractor can find out prices from the flooring supplier. Carpet is sold in square units. So, the floor's area tells how much carpet is needed. Baseboard surrounds the carpet along the bottom of the walls. It is sold in linear units. Perimeter is helpful here. Area and perimeter let the flooring supplier give correct prices to the contractor.

carpet cutter

1. How much carpet is needed to cover the floor of the living room?

2. The contractor will need to install baseboards along the bottom of the walls. How much baseboard will be needed?

3. Whoops! After the contractor calculates how much baseboard is needed, an important detail is discovered. There are two doorways! The doorways do not need to have baseboard. Each doorway is 1 yard wide. How much baseboard is needed now?

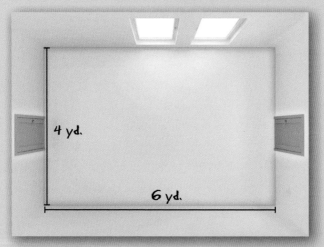

4 yd.

6 yd.

A circular saw cuts baseboard to exact measurements.

A contractor installs granite countertops

The clients are not finished with the bid yet! Now, they turn their attention to the kitchen. The countertops are in bad condition. They are stained from years of use. And there is a burn mark next to the stove where the previous owners set a hot pan. The clients want their counters upgraded with strong and stylish granite.

There are many types and colors of granite. The contractor chooses four options that would look good in the kitchen. One type of granite is shiny and black. It reminds the clients of the night sky. A second type is gray, with glittery specks that sparkle in the sunlight. The third option is dark brown, like a rich fudge brownie. The fourth option is a sandy beige. It reminds the clients of the beach. They have a hard decision to make!

granite samples

LET'S EXPLORE MATH

The clients really like the sandy beige granite. But they have not completely made up their minds. The contractor shows them a list of prices.

1. The kitchen counter is 10 feet long and 2 feet wide. If the clients choose the beige granite, how much will it cost?

2. How much would the clients save if they choose the shiny black granite instead?

Granite
SALE

Black Granite
$25 per sq. ft.

Gray Granite
$29 per sq. ft.

Brown Granite
$30 per sq. ft.

Beige Granite
$33 per sq. ft.

Buy It!

The contractor knows that a lot of materials will need to be purchased. Bundles of pipes, cans of paint, rolls of carpet, sections of baseboard, and slabs of granite are all on the shopping list. And the contractor will need tools, too. Nails, glue, paintbrushes, and masking tape are added to the list. All of these must be taken into account in the bid. If the contractor does not do so, all of the costs might not be covered. That might work out well for the clients. But, it would be bad for business. The contractor would lose money from the job.

This is when careful estimating is important. Doing this well helps clients understand the costs and work involved. And it helps contractors plan wisely.

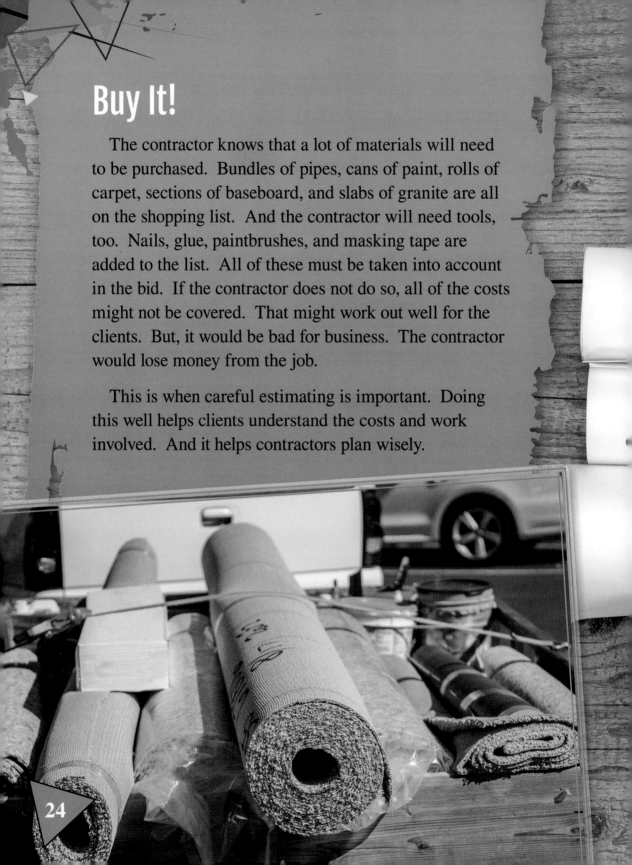

Kitchen Remodeling Project Checklist

SILVA
CONSTRUCTION

Appliances
- o Cooktop/range, gas or electric? _____
- o Dishwasher
- o Microwave
- o Oven(s)– gas or electric? _____
- o Range hood
- o Refrigerator
- o Trash Compactor
- o Disposal
- o Other _____
- o Keeping existing

Cabinetry
- o Natural wood, species: _____
- o Painted wood, color: _____
- o Combination: _____
- o Door style _____
- o Other: _____

Ceilings/Walls
- o Drywall
- o Plaster
- o Wood
- o Other _____
- o Keeping existing

Counter tops
- o Ceramic or granite tile
- o Granite Slabs
- o Laminate
- o Solid surface
- o Other _____

Flooring
- o Ceramic tile
- o Hardwood Species
- o Laminate
- o Vinyl
- o Other _____
- o Keep existing

Lighting
- o Ceiling fan/light(s)
- o Decorative
- o Recessed, general light
- o Task, under-cabinet
- o Other_____

Plumbing
- o Faucet
- o Garbage disposal
- o Sink
- o Other_____

Main Sink/Prep sink
- o Porcelain
- o Solid surface
- o Stainless
- o Self-rimming
- o Under-mount
- o Other_____

Additional requests
- o Windows _____
- o Doors _____
- o Skylights _____
- o Other _____

A Job Well Done

The contractor has taken all the measurements. Area and perimeter were used to help make the bid. Just to be on the safe side, the contractor checks the cost of all the materials and labor charges a second time. The last step is to give the clients the finished bid. It is up to the clients to decide.

The clients look at all of their options. But in the end, they make a wise choice. They think the bid is fair. And, they appreciate how detailed it is. It gives them confidence that the job will be done on time. They think the contractor can do quality work and give them everything they hope for. All that is left is for the contractor to buy the supplies and get started on the job!

Problem Solving

Word of mouth is a great way for contractors to get new clients. Ben wants some work done around his house. His neighbor just hired a contractor to do some work for her. She told Ben how pleased she was with the projects. So, Ben chose the same contractor to do some work in his backyard.

Ben wants the contractor to build a sandbox for his children. He already has 16 meters of new lumber for the sides of the sandbox. He would like the contractor to use this lumber instead of buying anything else. Ben's children want the sandbox to be either a rectangle or a square.

1. Make a list of all the rectangular-or square-shaped sandboxes that would have a perimeter of 16 meters.

2. Ben's children want the biggest sandbox possible. Find the area of each of the sandboxes in the proposal. Which has the largest area?

3. Which sandbox do you think would be best? Why?

Glossary

area—the amount of space covered by square units inside a two-dimensional shape

bid—a written estimate of the price to do a job

clients—people who pay other people or companies for services

contractors—people who manage construction projects

estimate—an educated guess about how much a job will cost

expenses—money spent regularly to pay for things

linear unit—a unit of measurement of length

perimeter—the distance around the outside of a shape

refinishing—putting a new coat on the surface of something

renovate—to make changes and repairs to an old house, building, room, etc. so that it is back in good condition

reputation—the common opinion that people have about someone or something

square units—units of measurement used to measure area

Index

Answer Key

Let's Explore Math

page 9:
1. 32 ft.
2. 120 sq. ft.
3. Area is measured in squares. So, area uses square units and not linear units.

page 17:
1. 112 ft.
2. Responses will vary. Example: Finding the perimeter of the lawn is different from finding the perimeter of a rectangle because the lawn does not have two sets of equal sides; the lawn has more than four sides. It is similar because the lengths of all of sides need to be added; it is measured in linear units.

page 19:
1. 18 sq. m
2. Yes; Two coats will require 36 sq. m of paint, and the paint will cover 40 sq. m.
3. 18 m of molding; linear units

page 21:
1. 24 sq. yd.
2. 20 yd.
3. 18 yd.

page 23:
1. $660
2. $160

Problem Solving

1. 1 m by 7 m; 2 m by 6 m; 3 m by 5 m; 4 m by 4 m
2. 7 sq. m; 12 sq. m; 15 sq. m; 16 sq. m. The 4 m by 4 m sandbox has the greatest area.
3. Answers will vary but may include: The 4 m by 4 m sandbox is best because it has the greatest area. It is a square, and other choices might be long and narrow.